QUARANTINED THOUGHTS

Jean-Sebastien Surena

Zara,

Thank you so much for supporting. Excited for your poetry journey!

—JEAN

QUARANTINED THOUGHTS
Copyright © 2021 Jean-Sebastien Surena

All rights reserved. This book or parts thereof may not be reproduced or used in any manner whatsoever without the express written permission of the publisher except for the use of brief quotations in a book review.

Jean-Sebastien Surena
Howard Beach, NY 11414
jeanthejournal@gmail.com

www.jeansurena.com

ISBN: 978-1-7370588-2-3

Library of Congress Control Number: 2021907417

Cover art by Bianca Monteiro
bnvmonteiro@gmail.com

Printed in the United States of America

First printing edition in 2021.

A Letter to the Reader

Dear Reader,

I am incredibly grateful to you for taking the time to read Quarantined Thoughts. The words within this book have been burning at the back of my mind since I wrote them; many are words that I refer back to when I'm in need of encouragement or peace. I hope that it can bring similar comfort and healing to those who read it.

To honor my late mother, one of the recurring figures in this book, a portion of Quarantined Thoughts' proceeds will be going to The Association for Frontotemporal Degeneration (AFTD). This will be a small step, but my first one in learning how I can use my voice to make the world a better place.

I'd like to say a heartfelt thank you for choosing to flip through the pages of my mind. As you make your way through my words, I only have one request – allow yourself to feel. Feel the pages, the rhythm, and your emotions. And if you must, allow yourself to fall, just as I did.

Warmest regards,

Jean

*To my mom,
who first put a book in my hand,
and would have been the first
to have this one in hers*

*and to you,
Thank you.*

CONTENTS

BLOOMLESS SPRING _____ 13

MADNESS IN SUMMER _____ 25

AS WE FALL _____ 43

COLDEST WINTER _____ 59

INTRODUCTION

Twenty-twenty, what a year you have been. Unrelenting chaos swallowed our world whole, giving birth to a new reality.

I've tried to put into words what 2020 meant to me, time and time again. And each time, I could not do it justice; so I opted to let my thoughts do the speaking.

Beyond this point, you will find pages scarred with battles and trials. My journal became a battlefield where I faced my identity, mental health, my mother's illness, and a world that – at times – felt like it was crumbling.

My heart, mind and soul could no longer bear to stay under quarantine, and I hope you enjoy their first foray beyond the confines of my journal.

P.S. *If you haven't heard or said it yet today, you are loved and you are worthy of love.*

BLOOMLESS SPRING

Planted seeds, colorless leaves, a chill courses through us on this summer's eve. For all the flowers that never got to bloom.

THE BEAST AND I, PART I

It coils around my neck
Threatening to sever
my consciousness
from the need to come correct

Its hold tightens
as I lose my grip
I need something to grab
before I flip my shit
Neither of us deserve this
But on some days
I question how we co-exist

3.26.2020

ON THE LINE

Keep me on the line
between facing the world
and facing myself

For just a little bit

Let me face you
Covered by hands
streaked with blue

Sing me a tune
Ballpoint scratches
Encapsulated truths

Hold me in your arms
until I know what to do,
until I can stand up on my own
and push myself through

4.26.2020

THE BEAST AND I, PART II

Trapped
The beast and I

Gasping for air
My neck's wrapped

Every day
Its hunger grows
Or it loses control

We are
Running out of time

How long until
One of us snaps

4.26.2020

DOUBLE STANDARDS

How many?
How many body bags
until they're satisfied

News that another one of us has died
has long become normalized
Black kids raised,
or raising
Deprived of the right
to untainted life
Having to be exposed early
to the unfairness of the world
Lest they end up in the back of a squad car
for not hitting some invisible bar

Double standards
We must stand under and understand
Rising above
apparently wasn't made for the colored man
Someone should let them know
we have other plans

5.6.2020

UNBROKEN

I'm angry
Livid, even
At people
At the world
At myself

Because I feel powerless
against the other two

Who decided
that our lives were worth less than yours
You like to point us to all the open doors
The same ones you had to "struggle to"
Then you slam it on our foot
when we try to go through

I'm angry

The system they said protects us all
played by people with the gall
to watch as we continue to fall
for standing a little too tall

No right to use the God-given spine
in my back
Unless I want to hear the proverbial
whip crack
Or worst case, hear the gun strap snap
Before it all goes black

I'm angry
We've been stepped on,
choked, shot, hunted, locked up
"Well it wouldn't have happened if you backed up"
Standing our ground,
a license to be shot up

I'm tired

Of seeing my brothers and sisters
on the pavement and in the dirt
Seeing my people cry and hurt
Shedding tears over people we've never met
because they were one of us
One wrong step and it could have been us
Our friends, families, our kids

I'm tired

Of having to conditionally earn respect
and human decency,
when others get it with the skin on their back
Having to walk a tightrope,
neck bound by a tight leash
Left alone to fight each
and every obstacle thrown our way

I'm tired

Of being entertainment
A victim
A casualty
A quota
A body

But you will not make me tired
of being Black

5.6.2020

COLORBLIND

"Not everything is about race"
What is it about then?
See, my mind can comprehend
a deeply rooted evil passed down for centuries
From white hand to white hand
It is disturbing
but I comprehend

What I cannot understand
is how one can defend
the actions of those intent
on bringing about our end

We, too, are the people they're meant to protect
But instead, we get brothers crushed,
knees on their necks
Gasping for air,
begging for help
Receiving disrespect

If it's not about race then
help me connect
the dots
What's at play here

What's the bigger plot?
What reason justifies
my people getting shot

You have all the answers
until a question is asked
Touting them as fact
Well, the fact of the matter is
we live in a country with a tax for being black
levied in amounts we'll never get back

To live without race in mind
is a choice to be blind to the inequalities,
injustices, and suffering facing my people
We are drained
emotionally, mentally, and spiritually
But we will not sit idly by
while you shovel us your crap
to try and cover up your tracks

We've been robbed of four hundred years
but it's stopping at that

5.27.2020

MADNESS IN SUMMER

My descent began with a mirror, a pen, and a journal.
It would not see its end.

ANCESTRAL TEARS

I cry for the ancestors
Born under the white man's boot
To 400 years later, look down
and see the white man shoot
sons and daughters of sons
staring down the barrels of guns
Feet caught in webs that are spun
for entertainment and fun

I cry for the ancestors
who knew we were destined for more
They put the hinges on doors
to watch us knocked to the floor
just a few inches off

But the ancestors knew
That black don't crack,
despite the scars on their backs
We'll take back what is ours
They planted the seeds
And we will grow the flowers

6.20.2020

IF THE BLACK MAN SUCCEEDS

I've come to a realization,
If the black man succeeds
there's no need for civilization
Caution to the wind
We can't win
with those fiends

They'll walk freely
Lack of burdens
straightening their backs
Can you imagine that?!

Young melanated queens
holding the world in between
the palm of their hands
Looking over their domain
and conquerable lands

And the young black men
Walking down the street
without a care in the world,
No fear as far as the eyes can see

I can see it so vividly

and I can't stand it
How can we give over the world
to those damned bandits
The thought is so outlandish
Our reign has been outstanding
Oppression breaking their backs
until they're not standing

If the black man succeeds
There will be no need for me
No one will kneel for me
My throne will be returned to a chair
and not a soul will even care
So don't you dare

Please.

6.20.2020

LONG-FORM RAMBLE, PART I

This is… underwhelming
I expected   fireworks
An explosion
Kabooms followed by kaplows
All I'm left with is

Ow; it hurts

Lost form, losing
       form
In this place, a foreign space
Seeking to re-discover
what was never mine
But I attributed the trademarks of my mind

Claimed, soul, making claims
to be whole
Claims? Aren't I…
whole?

This could be a rabbit hole

                                  Don't do it
                            That's not your goal

What is?
This is me
Hasn't this always been about
being me?
Telling you what I see
Or what I think I'd be like
if I'd be
in your shoes

                                                                     That's true

But whose shoes am I really after
Is that up to me?
Do I get to choose?

I feel like I want all of them
The ones that slip right on
A perfect fit
Where Cinderella ain't got shit on me

But I also want the clunky ones
Difficult, uncomfortable
A step-sister shunned
Not fitting in her own home
Living with family
But feeling so alone

That's what I want to capture
Moments come, and moments gone
Inner thoughts
Deepest wants

                                        Then do it
                                  What is stopping you?
                              You sit before a blank page
                                Not a thing in your way
                                    And you complain
                              That you can't find your way
                        There is nothing for you to find
                            The lines are merely a guide

But even that can be ignored

                          Don't sit in front of a canvas
                                  Paintbrush in hand
                                    With infinite color
Only to say you don't know where to begin
                                      Pick up your pen
                                  And douse the paper

                                  So much lies within
                                  It has to come out
                    Make your way to the mountaintop

                                                And shout

AAAAHHHHHHHHH

                                           How did that feel?

Like I want to take it off the paper

                                           Well, one day soon,
                                      I want you to do just that
                                    Bring that shout to reality
                                    As you sit atop the world
                                    Let your voice be heard

But what if they don't listen?

                                                     They will?

But if they don't?

                                                  They will
                              Only you decide who They are
                                      You alone choose
                               And once you understand that
                                      They will listen

How can you understand
Something I don't?
Do you not pull your wisdom from me?

                          I pull my wisdom from he
                    Who taught your baby self to breathe
                      I am beyond your experiences
                    But I observe and absorb them all
                              I am the failsafe
                      Here to catch you if you fall

                      I am giving you my strength
                          You have been so strong
          You've fought well and you have made it here
                          Now say it loud and clear

I am here

6.4.2020

EPILOGUE

When my last day comes
Will I dutifully accept?
Content that I've lived
with no regrets
Ready for what's next
Set to go

Or will I be clawing?
My mind too far in
a place that's not foreign
Disappointed with my imperfection
Not because it exists
but due to my lack of acceptance
My aim to perfect every sentence
Sentencing myself to pain
even with nothing left to gain

Or will it be a day
much like today
My thoughts wavering between what I've done
and would do
What I haven't
but should do

Before it ends
and I conclude
to nothing

Unaware that the end is soon coming

8.9.2020

LONG-FORM RAMBLE, PART II

Silently pleading
Suppressed sobs
Weeping
She calls out to me
"You're losing yourself," she whispers
Her eyes are closed
but she stares intently into my soul
The hold she has is untold

She sees
desolate lands
Ravaged
by a desperate man
who wants for both sides
Balance and chaos

He keeps finding the light
but he casts it aside
In with the waves
out with the tides
Receding
Regressing
Proceeding with caution
Then falling off the side

with reckless abandon

Never alone but abandoned
The voices they fight
Me, myself, and I
I don't listen most of the time
I find it easiest
To bury myself out of sight
Fight or flight
In danger

But I've no fight left in me

There's a question
Unanswered
I was searching
Now I've forgotten
what it was

The demons were lurking
Sharpening their claws
So she calls
Praying that I answer

Living on Do Not Disturb
yet consistently disturbed

I'm hurting but I refuse to face
the wound
She begs me to look before
the wound brings on my doom

7.12.2020

HEMORRHAGE

My darkest moments
were when you brought me
Into the depths of your despair
Glimpses of the demons
terrorizing your soul
Enough to make my blood run cold
How did you hold on
for so many years
Battling yourself, your fears
Hiding your tears

From me
For me
For us

Torturing myself with an ever-growing
list of questions
that will never get answered

8.26.2020

THE LIGHT THAT DID NOT SHINE

I had hoped
that I could be your light
You'd hear my voice,
feel my presence
right by your side
And the darkness would dissipate
The fog would lift, the veil cast aside
You'd open your eyes
and you'd be back home
No longer alone
in the abyss of your thoughts
Sleepless nights fraught with nightmares
You can no longer distinguish
from reality
Your moments of rest
invaded by memories and anguish

"I've lived a bad life,"
you said so many times
A narrator summarizing
at the story's end
You had finished the book
while we were still flipping pages
We waited for the next chapter

for what felt like ages

Oblivious to the fact that it was done
and all we had left were distorted reruns

8.26.2020

AS WE FALL

The weight of my mind became unbearable. I could not lie still, and I could not stand. So I fell.

THE PORCH

We sit in silence
Cool September night
The air is filled with laughter and chatter
but we don't join the chorus
We sit on the steps,
smoke coiling its way around our bodies,
rising to join the clouds
Dissipating
Somewhere in between,
our thoughts continue to rise
Hoping we can reach the destination
that the smoke could not
Distant sirens snap us out of our reverie
Our eyes meet
We share a laugh
A joke untold
Alone, yet together
in our own little worlds

9.20.2020

STASIS

I've spent quite some time
in fear of the long form
The shorter thoughts come easier
They're simple, less room for mistakes
and if I mess up,
they're forgettable

My longer pieces have previously
carried the weight of my heart
I assert myself with conviction
"This is what I believe in,
you will sit here and listen"

But most of the time
that's not how I am
I hesitate, I stumble
I question myself
then I question my responses

Uncertainty grips me
in its freezing fist
so short bursts are all I'm capable of
Before I'm stuck again
Frozen in stasis

9.22.2020

WHY DO I WRITE?

I am
searching for the origin
Looking for something within
but without a location
Untraceable
The details escape me

The memories… they're hazy, images
of a younger self having no other way
of professing his love, feeling
all he can do is write it
so it does not escape his lips

Another me, taking a stand
Pen in hand, engraving the words
That roll from his tongue
to bolster his voice
Singing praises of the motherland,
enhanced by strokes of ink

Yet another me, whispering ink-laced
secrets onto blank pieces of paper
Secrets that go from the
subconscious to the fingertips

Not daring to so much as scratch
the roof of my mouth for fear
that I'll find out

The present me, posing questions
Hoping they can't be answered
Attempting to connect inter-dimensional
dots on one plane
Chasing the impossible between the lines
Where is the origin
What do I do this for?

9.22.2020

NOTE TO SELF

We've reached the end of yet another journey, another journal. #3 is officially in the books. (Ha, get it?) As with all great endings, it is also a beginning – Journal #4, re-discovering and re-defining my long form, and hopefully much more. I feel at peace, as much as I can, at least, with mommy in the hospital. I am enjoying the process of learning about poetry and learning about myself. We're a bit over a year since the start of Journal #1, and I'm discovering that there's still so much more to learn, experience and experiment with. I have had many moments where I've doubted myself, and I'm sure that these are not behind me completely, but I need to remember the days like today, where I really feel that I have a voice worth hearing, and that I didn't pick up this pen for nothing. I love you.

9.23.2020

DO NOT DISTURB

My phone sits
Silent
A seductress with the unspoken word

It beckons with no hands
and a blank stare
Calls for my name without uttering a word

Do Not Disturb

Is it for me, or for you?
You have not moved an inch
But my personal space
has been invaded

It's suffocating
The black of your screen,
the entrance to an abyss
void of happy endings

                                          Keep your mind off

Eyes boring into my soul
My own

I've found my reflection
peering back from the darkness

                                                Keep your mind off

It stares intently
It wants to consume me
I need to know
what's on the other side

                                                Keep your mind off

My hands tremble
as they unfurl
Formerly clenched
fists becoming undone

                                          Keep your mind off. Please.

My mind is no longer
in control
Instinct has taken over
I pick it up
The sweat that sits
Upon my palm threatens
to allow it to fall

I tighten my grip
We've come this far

Its screen now sits
with antagonizing indifference
to my ravenous pursuit
for answers, for calm
Lifetimes pass within the next second
as the screen flickers to life

"No new notifications."

9.23.2020

MISCALCULATION

This was not adding up.
I checked my work,
nothing seemed to be off.
I re-read the instructions,
for what felt like the hundredth time.
"Which of these could be values of x."
The same 8 words and 28 letters
I'd seen when I last read them.

A sharp snap.

My head swiveled to my pencil,
a piece of 0.7 mm graphite
broken and motionless at its tip.
I absentmindedly drove its end into my book
in my bout of frustration.

But that was not the sound I heard.
No, this sound was… closer —
much closer.
Its echo still rang about in my head.

A single droplet of water made its way
from my eye,

down the side of my nose,
along my cheek, past the corner of my mouth
and onto my sleeve.
Then another, yet another,
several more followed.

What an odd feeling,
the floodgates had opened up,
and I still did not have my answer.
How in the world would I check my work
and read the instructions now.

But this was never really about math, was it?

9.24.2020

RIGHT HAND (BEDSIDE, PART I)

One, two, three, four, five
I count again
One, two, three, four, five,
the fingers of your right hand
gripping the side of your bed
You look into my eyes,
your mouth moves but no sound comes out
I rattle off a series of questions,
you respond with a series of head shakes and nods
Eventually, you look away
and shake your head at something in the distance

    Distant

A faraway look settles in your eyes
Pain
Suffering every day,
unable to explain your feelings
Misunderstood, even now, when you can
no longer stand on your own
My heart aches at the thought
of how alone you must feel

9.26.2020

VITAL SIGNS (BEDSIDE, PART II)

With every beep,
every twitch
every gasp
my heart drops
Leaving me suspended
for a moment
Away from reality
Then it snaps up,
hand reaching for yours,
asking if you're okay
Hoping the last beep I heard isn't the one
that will send nurses and doctors
sprinting through the doors
as they do in the movies
Giving me a front row seat
to the world premiere
of my worst nightmare

9.26.2020

FINAL DAYS (BEDSIDE, PART III)

Every time I ask if you're okay,
you give me an insistent nod
Followed by shallow pants,
ragged breaths
and pained facial expressions
I ask again
Another nod
Maintaining a brave face
as you have for most of your life
A life that, through to the end,
showed you nothing but pain

The sounds —
They worry you too
Darting eyes
Each new one
catches you by surprise
"What does this all mean?"
you seem to ask
Your face echoing
The same question
that's been tormenting my mind

10.3.2020

COLDEST WINTER

"On lonely nights, I start to fade. Her love is a thousand miles away." – *Kanye West*

EULOGY

I wish we could have shared
One more dance
One more joke
One more laugh
One more song
One more lesson
One more hug
One more kiss
One more day
One more life

I wish I could go back and tell you
You didn't have to worry so much
You didn't have to fight so hard
You didn't have to work so hard for us
I wish you were able to step back
And realize how much you did for us
I wish you saw the beautiful children you raised
I wish we spent more time together
Learning about each other
Instead of learning to grow apart

You never stopped loving me
I hope you know I never stopped either

I wish I could tell you that
And see you smile and nod
Telling me you love me too

I'm going to miss you
More than you will ever know
But I know you will be watching over me
I spent a lot of my life pushing myself to succeed
So that I could make you and dad happy,
Thinking "I'm only doing this because you want me to"

This time, I'm going to do this for us
I'm going to make you so so proud
By making myself proud
And living life to the fullest
Like I know you wish you had

I will be on top of the world
So you can see me better
So Manmita can see me better
So Tatie Maryse can see me better
And you will share with them
A dance, a smile, a laugh, a song, a hug, a life

I love you, always.

10.13.2020

LOST ART

I am terrified
of losing the art within me
We live in such
turbulent times
The uncertainty is troubling,
and hurting my creative drive
Ability to derive emotion from pain
I'm overloaded

Are there too many choices
or am I losing my voice
Throat closing up,
head banging, scratching, lost
Just looking for words

I used to talk a lot,
saying I want to be heard
But how can the world hear
if I can't hear myself

I am terrified
of losing the art within me
We live in such turbulent times

Depriving the world of my voice
Would be a terrible crime
So I'll keep trying

10.24.2020

LONG-FORM RAMBLE, PART III

It might be time
for another long-form ramble
My head is in a scramble to find
some semblance of its former normalcy
It feels scrambled,
no sunny side to be found, up nor down

These past few weeks,
I've had an inexplicable gloom
looming over my shoulders
Shoulders and a body I'd learned to diligently train,
now being thrown into disarray
Emotions I had learned to display
returning to the holes they once hid in

I am in dissonance with myself
and I can't find the unturned key
I can't place my finger on the trigger
that has caused all of this
It could very well be that my subconsciousness
is processing something I've yet to grasp
and it's such an undertaking
that there is little power left for me

But if so, it is actively breaking me in the process
I feel trapped in old routines and processes
I'd long broken free from
The old, rusted chains of despair are finding their links and climbing
up to my ankles and wrists
But I need to resist
I can resist, I must resist
I'm better than this

My growth has not been for naught
Growing doesn't mean you'll never end up
in certain situations again
It means that if you do,
you will already know how to get out
You will be better equipped to face new challenges
and you are —
I am
My growth is not a facade
I am different, I am wiser
I can get through this
I will get through this

12.4.2020

Spring will come again.

ABOUT THE AUTHOR

Jean-Sebastien Surena, Jean for short, is a tech consultant born and (mostly) raised in Queens, NY. He likes to moonlight as a poet during his off hours. He first discovered poetry during a homework assignment in the sixth grade, where he wrote a love poem deemed (by his teacher) to be "too passionate to share with the class."

Jean began taking his writing more seriously in college, where he wrote and performed pieces on race, identity and relationships. He graduated as the Salutatorian of Baruch College's Class of 2019; after his graduation, he rewarded himself with his first physical journal, and has been tattooing pages since. He has occasionally shared his pieces on Instagram, under the handle @jeanthejournal, but *Quarantined Thoughts* is his first published work.

Beyond poetry and technology, Jean is a serial dabbler in theater, acting, photography, dancing, fashion, games and binge watching shows. He hopes to add his name to a long list of impactful artists hailing from New York, while bringing his own unique perspective, language and lived experience. You can chat with Jean via his Instagram, through his website at https://jeansurena.com, or by email: jeanthejournal@gmail.com.

ACKNOWLEDGMENTS

The warmest of thank yous to Bianca for an absolutely gorgeous cover. There is almost nothing that compares to the moment when I held my first copy of *Quarantined Thoughts* in my hands, and was graced by the cover in physical form.

Thank you to Suswana and Jashima for helping me navigate this incredibly daunting self-publishing world. You are a powerhouse team and your skills and support made me feel like I could accomplish anything.

Thank you to the friends who have helped keep me sane through this pandemic – there are too many to name, but you know who you are. To Anna, thank you for listening to me read my poetry for countless hours, and giving me confidence that my voice was worth hearing; you made this all possible.

A special thank you to my dad and my sister. There is no way to fully express the depth of what we have been through together in life and over this past year but thank you for never faltering in your support.

And I must reiterate, thank YOU for reading.

Over the next few pages, I've left some space for you to share your own quarantined thoughts. I'd love to know what carried you through the seasons of our year in quarantine. Feel free to share them with me via social media @jeanthejournal!

QUARANTINED THOUGHT #1
BLOOMLESS SPRING
DATE: /   /

QUARANTINED THOUGHT #2
MADNESS IN SUMMER
DATE: /   /

QUARANTINED THOUGHT #3
AS WE FALL
DATE: /   /

QUARANTINED THOUGHT #4
COLDEST WINTER
DATE: /   /

Made in the USA
Middletown, DE
30 July 2023